İstanbul: City of
Memories and Hopes

İSTANBUL
BÜYÜKŞEHİR
BELEDİYESİ

İstanbul: City of Memories and Hopes

Project Management: Ali Pekşen
Editorial Contribution: Zümrüt Alp _ Zeynep Avcı _ Susanne Fawler _ Ayça İnce

ISBN: 975-6857-90-0

Cover: Altuğ Şahin

İstanbul, 2005

For Information Address: İstanbul Büyükşehir Belediyesi
                        Saraçhane-Fatih/İstanbul-Turkey
                        Tel: +90 (212) 455 14 00
                        www.ibb.gov.tr

© Bilgi İletişim Grubu Yayıncılık Müzik Yapım ve Haber Ajansı Ltd.Şti.
                        İnönü Caddesi No: 28 Kuştepe
                        Şişli 34387 İstanbul-Turkey
                        Tel +90 (212) 311 60 00
                        Fax +90 (212) 347 10 11

Photography: İldem Akçakaya _ Alper Akçay _ Yasin Baran _ Bertan Başaran _ İhsan Derman _ Aylin Dinçer _
Onur Eroğlu _ Engin Gerçek _ Fırat Giraygil _ Alişan Özkan _ Burak Pekakcan _ Ali Pekşen _ Ebru Sile

Design: Altuğ Şahin
Technical Management: Volkan Çetin
Technical Assistant: Bora Yüce

Printer and Binder: Mas Matbaacılık A.Ş
                   Dereboyu Cad. Zağra İş Merkezi
                   B Blok No:1 Maslak / İstanbul -Turkey
                   Tel: +90 (212) 285 11 96
                   Fax: +90 (212) 276 59 55
                   info@masmat.com.tr

CONTENTS

ISTANBUL: CITY OF MEMORIES & HOPES

"I COULD NO LONGER TELL IF I WAS IN BYZANTIUM, CONSTANTINOPOLIS OR İSTANBUL. I REALIZED THAT I MADE A TRIP WHERE I TRAVERSED THREE CIVILIZATIONS AND THREE PERIODS AT THE SAME TIME."

UMBERTO ECO

İstanbul, the melting pot of civilizations for centuries...

İstanbul, the cozy home of different religions and sects...

İstanbul, the shining star shedding light on journeys to different cultures...

İstanbul, the beloved mother, sheltering the history and future of the modern world in tandem...

We are at the turn of a new century. As time goes by following its own course, history reveals itself in complex equations in İstanbul. Wandering around the town, you will hear secrets being whispered to your ear, waiting to be discovered. Yet, she may be reluctant to show her true face. Is it possible to see what lies beneath only by viewing the jewels on her, the historical monuments? Well, I would recommend you to have a real experience in her streets in daylight and enjoy the jewels of history amazingly having a life of their own. At this point, maybe, though partly, she will reveal you the bridges linking past with present. I say partly, because the heart of this city, consisting of multicultural art, trade and social tissues is not easy to discover in short trips. Such a mystical experience will take a whole life, at least a couple of months or a couple of seasons to see her in different attires. And, you are one of those fortunate guests invited to meet this city of conception.

One feels uneasy with words when it comes to describe her. Perhaps, a snapshot in an album of İstanbul is a way out. In these photographs, the multicolored structure of the city is reflected on its people who will take you to follow the traces of three civilizations and three religions at home. You will see the spirit, the memories and the historical buildings captured in the frames. Now, it's time to be alone with the photographs of contemporary İstanbul. Shots of modern life through a great history, something to remind future generations of the birth of a century.

Now please turn the page to start your journey.

Arch.Dr. Kadir TOPBAŞ

Mayor of İstanbul Metropolitan Municipality

İstanbul: City of Memories & Hopes

This collection is not a complete album, but rather an impression of modern İstanbul with a historic backdrop. It reflects the city through scenes of the streets and its inhabitants.

In this album, the reader will come across two İstanbuls: One, a romantic landscape with palaces, mosques, churches, synagogues and "yalıs" along the sparkling Bosphorus, the other, a lively metropolis of more than 12 million-which at times camouflages this romantic landscape with impressive skyscrapers and busy traffic.

The inhabitants reflect the other dichotomy of İstanbul: the Ottoman, "cosmopolitan" of different religions and ethnicities that subsists today with symbols of the "brotherhood of civilizations" at every corner of the city, and the contemporary "cosmopolitan" of immigrants, enriched by Anatolian lives while threatened by unplanned urban developments.

We believe that the decisiveness of the people and of the local government will overcome the challenges posed by these dichotomies and transform İstanbul into one of the cultural capitals of the world.

There are two İstanbuls: one of memories and one of hopes.

The pictures will tell more than words...

CONSTANTLY BUSY

URBAN

ONE OF THE FIRST METROPOLS IN HISTORY, İSTANBUL IS THE CENTER OF ATTRACTION IN TURKEY. THE CITY HAS BEEN EXPANDING DRAMATICALLY SINCE THE 50'S, CURRENTLY AT AN ESTIMATED 700,000 IMMIGRANTS PER YEAR. TODAY, WITH A POPULATION OVER 12 MILLION, İSTANBUL IS HOME TO ONE IN SIX TURKS.

İSTANBUL CONTINUES TO BE A CITY THAT CREATES ITS OWN HISTORY. ALONGSIDE HISTORIC İSTANBUL, ONE FINDS A VIBRANT NIGHT LIFE WITH HIP BARS AND CLUBS, FLASHY EXECUTIVE RYHTHM, MALLS, AND HAUTE CUISINE. THE ENRICHED ARTS SCENE ACTS AS A PLATFORM WHERE THE OTTOMAN AND BYZANTINE HERITAGE MESHES WITH EUROPEAN TRENDS AND IS AN INTEGRAL PART OF THE CITY'S COSMOPOLITAN NATURE. LAST BUT NOT LEAST IS THE BOSPHORUS – İSTANBUL'S EVER-BUSY BODY OF WATER ALIVE WITH SHIPS AND FERRIES LINKING EUROPE AND ASIA – THAT IS THE SPINE OF THIS CULTURAL AND URBAN HUSTLE&BUSTLE.

MINARET: THE SIGNATURE OF THE OLD TOWN.

SUNDAY ON THE ROCKS.

11

12 THE NIGHT IS STILL YOUNG.

BOATS: A DELICACY OF TRANSPORTATION.

YOU CAN SAIL AND DINE ON ONE OF THE RENOVATED BOATS.

TIME SLOWS AND COOLS DOWN ON THE BOSPHORUS.

15

THE NEWEST OF THE FOUR BRIDGES ON THE GOLDEN HORN.

THE SECOND BOSPHORUS BRIDGE, CONSTRUCTED IN 1988.

FERRY BOATS, PASSENGER BOATS, "CAIQES" (SMALL FISHING BOATS) AND LARGE SHIPS NAVIGATE THE BOSPHORUS IN A MIRACULOUS HARMONY.

MANY A SHIP LOOMS IN THE PORT OF İSTANBUL CARRYING PEOPLE TO DIFFERENT SEAS.

THE COLOSSAL SHIP SILENTLY AWAITS DEPARTURE.

THE MAGICAL TRIP BETWEEN ASIA AND EUROPE TAKES ONLY 20 MINUTES.

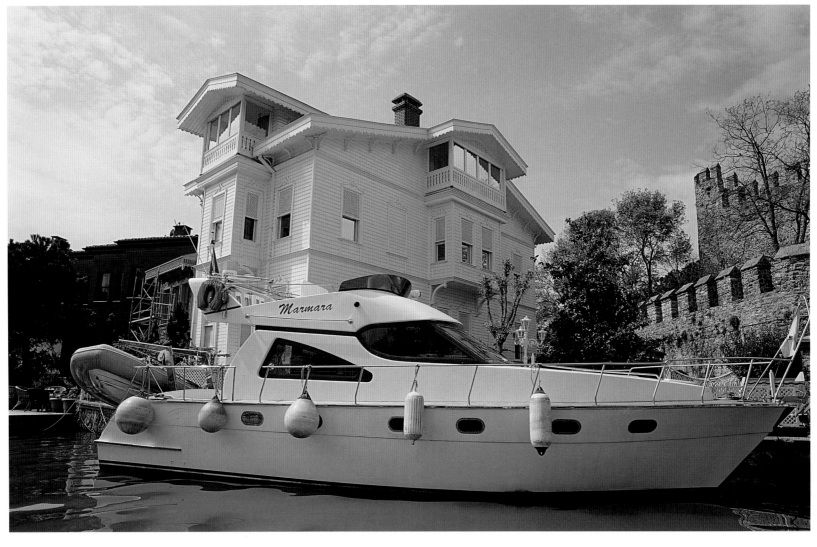

SOME HAVE THEIR OWN WAYS OF TRANSPORTATION.

"YALI": OLD MANSIONS ON THE SHORES OF THE BOSPHORUS.

23

24 THE KIOSKS OF THE OLD OTTOMAN PALACES ARE FLATTERED BY TULIP BEDS IN THE SPRINGTIME.

THE JUDAS TREES SURROUNDING AN OLD MANSION REVEAL THE TYPICAL BEAUTY OF THE BOSPHORUS.

 SİRKECİ TRAIN STATION: A RENOWN STOP OF THE ORIENT EXPRESS.

BUILT AT THE END OF THE 19TH CENTURY, THE HAYDARPAŞA TRAIN STATION IS A GATE TO ANATOLIA.

28 SEAGULLS AND THE SUNKEN FISHING BOAT.

ONE OF THE FUN CHOICES TO CROSS BOSPHORUS IS THE CAR FERRY.

AFTER A LONG AND EXHAUSTING DAY THE PASSENGER FERRIES REST AT GALATA HARBOR.

SOMETIMES HEAVY SNOW STOPS THE TRANSPORTATION ON THE BOSPHORUS.

31

HISTORIC HAYDARPAŞA HIGH SCHOOL BUILDING ACCOMMODATES THE MARMARA UNIVERSITY.

ESCAPE FROM THE FINAL EXAM STRESS.

MANY OF THE MANSIONS, WHICH ONCE SERVED OTTOMAN ARISTOCRACY AND "PASHAS" ARE RENOVATED AND HAVE BECOME NEW RESIDENCES.

THE BEAUTIFUL DISTRICT OF TARABYA ON THE EUROPEAN SHORE OF THE BOSPHORUS TAKES ITS
NAME FROM THE WORD "TERAPIA" OR THERAPY.

35

ANKARA TRAINS ARRIVING AT HAYDARPAŞA STATION BRING TO MIND THE WORDS OF A GREAT TURKISH POET: "THE BEST PART OF BEING IN ANKARA IS THE TRIP BACK TO İSTANBUL".

THE CLOCK TOWER OF THE FORMER HAYDARPAŞA HIGH SCHOOL.

SITUATED IN THE POPULAR TAKSİM SQUARE, THE ATATÜRK CULTURAL CENTER HOSTS NATIONAL AND INTERNATIONAL PERFORMANCES.

THE "TRAMVAY" RUNS BETWEEN THE TWO ENDS OF İSTİKLAL CADDESİ, ONE OF THE MOST ANIMATED STREETS OF THE CITY.

39

IS HE ALREADY A "TOP MAN" OR IS HE JUST ENTHUSIASTIC TO BECOME ONE?

A DOME OF TRADITION STANDS TALL BEHIND AN ITEM OF MODERN MARKETING.

AN OLD WAY OF MARKETING AND SELLING WITH A HUMBLE BUT DEMANDING SMILE.

A SERIOUS CITIZEN OF İSTANBUL.

44

ATATÜRK, FATHER OF TURKS STILL SUPPORTS THE TURKS, HE PASSED AWAY IN 1938. THIS VENDOR MAKES MONEY OUT OF HIS POSTERS.

THE TURKISH WOMAN WHO GAINED THE RIGHT TO ELECT AND TO BE ELECTED FAR BEFORE THE WOMEN
OF MANY EUROPEAN COUNTRIES THANKS TO ATATÜRK.

THE INTERIOR OF THE HISTORICAL BUILDING OF MARMARA UNIVERSITY.

MANY SHOPPING MALLS ENTERED THE DAILY LIFE OF İSTANBUL IN THE 90'S.

A VIEW OF THE HISTORICAL PENINSULA AND THE TOPKAPI PALACE.

THE MONUMENT IN TAKSİM SQUARE DECORATES THE HEART OF THE NEW CITY.

"MANAV": THE ART OF FRUIT EXHIBITION.

A WELL-KNOWN INTELLECTUAL RASİH NURİ İLERİ AND HIS FLAT: TREASURE OF POLITICAL MEMORIES.

52 THE OLD POWER PLANT CAN NO LONGER PRODUCE ELECTRICITY BUT IT WILL BE HOSTING AND
PRODUCING ART VERY SOON.

WORKS OF ART WILL BE EXHIBITED SIDE BY SIDE WITH THE MACHINARY AND THE EQUIPMENT OF
THE POWER PLANT WHEN İSTANBUL'S NEW MUSEUM AT SİLAHTARAĞA/GOLDEN HORN OPENS.

THE MODERN UNIVERSITIES OF İSTANBUL HARBOUR A DYNAMIC ACADEMIC ENVIRONMENT.

THESE UNIVERSITIES ESTABLISH A CULTURAL AND SCIENTIFIC COMMUNITY THAT PROMOTES
TOLERANCE AND RESPECT FOR DIVERSE LIFESTYLES, BELIEFS AND WAYS OF THINKING.

THIS IS A FOOTBALL CROWD, TENSION IS IN THE AIR.

AND THIS IS A POLITICAL MARCH. PEACEFUL AND RELAXED!

57

SPEED IS THE OBJECT, COLOR IS THE CHARACTER.

58

THIS IS A JOKE OF COURSE.

THE OLD ORTHODOX SCHOOL.

AND THE NEW NEIGHBORHOOD.

LYCÉE DE "GALATASARAY", ALSO GIVES ITS NAME TO A FAMOUS TURKISH SOCCER TEAM.

BEAUTIES OF OLD CITY

FEMININE

THEY ARE THE GRAND DAUGHTERS OF THE HITITE QUEEN PUDUHEPA, MOTHER GODDESS CYBELE, GODDESS ARTEMISIA, APHRODITE ANADYOMENE, TYCHE: THE GODDESS OF GOOD FORTUNE, QUEEN SINOPE, PRIESTESSES OF DEMETER, AND OF ALL THE OTHER WOMEN WHO HAVE LIVED IN ANATOLIA FOR 9,000 YEARS.

THEY EITHER WERE BORN IN İSTANBUL, OR THEY CAME FROM ANATOLIA AND FROM THRACE. THEY NOURISH İSTANBUL WITH THEIR ENERGY, WITH THEIR HOPES, WITH THEIR AFFECTION. THEY ARE THE WOMEN OF İSTANBUL, SISTERS AND BEAUTIES OF THIS ANCIENT TOWN.

ONE HAS TO THINK CAREFULLY AND PLAN THE FUTURE.

AN AFTERNOON BREAK. NO ONE KNOWS WHO BROKE THE RULE FIRST.

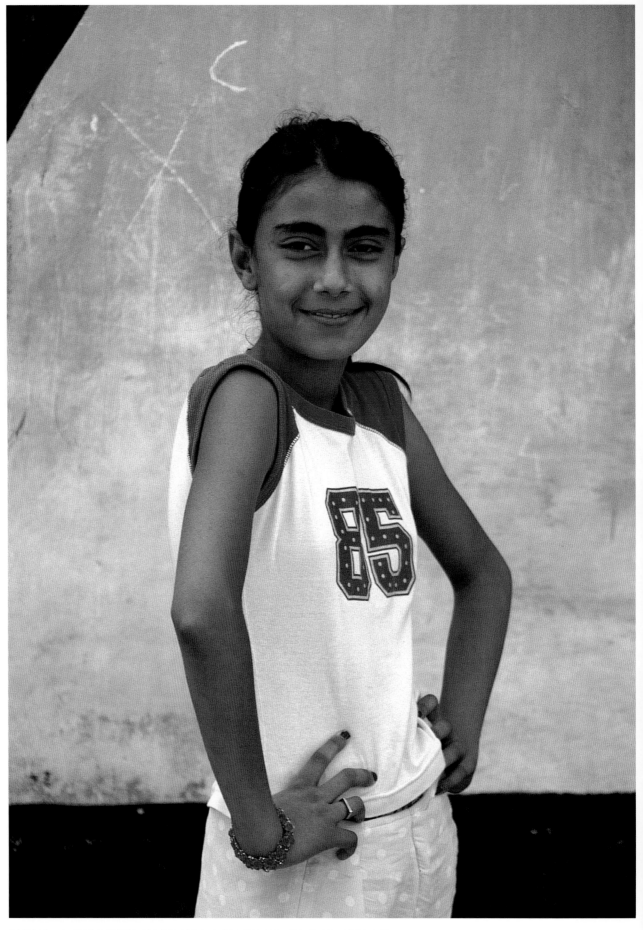

SHE IS 13, BUT SHE WANTS TO LOOK OLDER IN THE PICTURE.

"WOULD YOU LIKE SOME FLOWERS?"

TRADITIONAL FOOD PRESENTED BY A GLOBAL APPROACH.

FOREVER YOUNG.

70 TWINS? NO! SPARKLING GREETINGS.

THE BEST WAY TO CATCH UP WITH THEM IS TO LOOK LIKE THEM.

SHE HAS PLANS. HE IS CERTAINLY A PART OF HER PLANS.

"SHE PLAYS MUSIC WHILE I STUDY, HOW FAIR IS THAT?"

74 A WONDERFUL SHOPPING BREAK: FISH IS FRESH AND BREAD IS WARM.

EVERYBODY IS FREE TO DECIDE WHAT TO WEAR.

"WHATEVER SHE COOKS THERE... CAN I COOK IT AT HOME?"

76

A SUMMER BREEZE...

SHOPPING MALLS AND WOMEN... WHAT NEED IS THERE FOR MEN?

IF IT WERE "TOP WOMAN", WOULD THEY PASS SO QUICKLY?

THERE IS NO DOUBT THAT SHE WILL BE SMILING SOON.

THE PURSE IS SAFE; THE FILM WAS GOOD; WHAT'S THE WORRY?

ENTUSIASTIC ABOUT THE FUTURE.

THE BEST WAY TO OVERCOME EVERYTHING IS TO SMILE.

84 TODAY, IT IS HER TURN TO FISH.

SHE IS DONE FEEDING HER CHILDREN. IT IS TIME TO FEED THE PIGEONS.

85

BEFORE AND DURING THE RAMAZAN.

RELIGIOUS AND SECULAR

MYSTIC

"THERE, GOD AND HUMAN, NATURE AND ART ARE TOGETHER, THEY HAVE CREATED SUCH A PERFECT PLACE THAT IS VALUABLE TO SEE." ALPHONSE DE LAMARTINE'S POETIC LINES REVEAL HIS LOVE FOR İSTANBUL, THE ONLY CITY WHICH HAS BEEN A CAPITAL TO TWO CONSECUTIVE EMPIRES: CHRISTIAN AND ISLAMIC.

ANCIENT AND MODERN, RELIGIOUS AND SECULAR, ASIA AND EUROPE, MYSTICAL AND EARTHLY ALL COEXIST HERE. İSTANBUL IS A MEETING POINT FOR THE THREE ABRAHAMIC TRADITIONS. IT HAS A CULTURE THAT BRINGS TOGETHER THE BEST OF THE ORIENT AS WELL AS THE BEST OF THE WEST. ALL BELIEFS ARE WELCOME HERE. TODAY, THERE ARE 157 CHRISTIAN CHURCHES, 17 SYNAGOGUES AND 10 MONASTERIES IN İSTANBUL AND NEARLY 2000 MOSQUES. THANKS TO THE TOLERANCE OF THE OTTOMANS MAJORITY OF THE RELIGIOUS BUILDINGS FROM THE FORMER BYZANTINE PERIOD STILL STANDS TODAY.

88

THE BEYAZIT MOSQUE WAS BUILT AT THE BEGINNING OF THE 16th CENTURY. IT IS THE OLDEST IMPERIAL MOSQUE FROM THE OTTOMAN ERA. THE INTERIOR DESIGN IS A SIMPLIFIED VERSIAN OF THE ST. SOFIA.

FUNERALS OF THE MOST PROMINENT OF İSTANBUL'S CITIZENS ARE CARRIED OUT IN THE TEŞVİKİYE MOSQUE SITUATED IN THE CHIC NEIGHBORHOOD OF NİŞANTAŞI.

90   THE ORTAKÖY MOSQUE WAS BUILT AT THE END OF THE 19th CENTURY; ITS DECORATIONS TYPIFY THE BAROQUE INFLUENCE OF THE PERIOD. IT STANDS NEAR THE LIVELY ORTAKÖY SQUARE AND THE FIRST BOSPHORUS BRIDGE.

EVERYONE CAN ENTER A MOSQUE AND BREATH ITS SPIRITUAL AIR PROVIDED IT IS NOT PRAYER
TIME. VISITORS OF THE BLUE MOSQUE (SULTANAHMET) RELAX ON ITS CARPETS AND COLLECT
INVALUABLE MEMORIES.

92   THERE ARE MANY SYNAGOGUES IN İSTANBUL WHERE MEMBERS OF THE JEWISH COMMUNITY GATHER IN RELIGIOS RITUAL.

BUILT IN MEMORY OF THE ENGLISH SOLDIERS WHO DIED IN THE CRIMEAN WAR, THE CRIMEAN CHURCH IS STILL IN USE TODAY.

94

TULIP IS THE SYMBOL OF İSTANBUL AND OF THE GLORIOUS OTTOMAN PAST. IF THE PRIEST LIKES GARDENING, WHY NOT PLANT TULIPS IN THE ENTRANCE OF HIS CHURCH?

AN "İMAM" IS GETTING READY FOR PRAYER.

96   AN ORTHODOX PRIEST OF THE FENER PATRIARCHATE BEFORE A RELIGIOUS CEREMONY.

FINISHED BETWEEN 532 AND 537, DURING THE REIGN OF EMPEROR JUSTINIAN, ST. SOFIA IS ONE
OF THE OLDEST MONUMENTS OF İSTANBUL. IT SERVED MANY GENERATIONS AS TEMPLE AND
INFLUENCED GREAT ARCHITECTS SUCH AS SINAN AS ART.

98

THE CHURCH OF THE CHORA MONASTERY'S ORIGINAL STRUCTURE WAS COMMISSIONED BY THE HOLY THEODUS IN 534 DURING THE REIGN OF JUSTINIAN. IN THE 11th AND 12th CENTURIES, IT WAS REBUILT BY THE COMNENUS FAMILY AND DEDICATED TO CHRIST.

CONVERTED TO A MUSEUM IN THE 1940's KARİYE MÜZESİ (CHORA MUSEUM) UNDERWENT A
DECADE-LONG RESTAURATION. THE CLEANING REVEALED BOTH THE BREATHTAKING QUALITY OF
ITS MOSAICS, WHICH ARE IN REMARKABLY GOOD CONDITION.

99

THE BULGARIAN "IRON CHURCH" AND THE BUILDINGS OF THE ORTHODOX PATRIARCHATE
DOMINATE THE ANCIENT FENER DISTRICT ON THE SHORES OF GOLDEN HORN.

THE İMAM OF THE BLUE MOSQUE IS ALSO THE VOLUNTARY ADVISOR OF ALL VISITORS FROM
DIFFERENT BELIEFS AND THE INHABITANTS OF THE NEIGHBORHOOD.

THE ORTHODOX CHURCH IN FENER HAS BEEN AND STILL IS VISITED BY MANY GREEKS FROM ALL OVER THE WORLD. ITS SPLENDOR HASN'T CHANGED SINCE THE 17th CENTURY.

AN ORTHODOX PRIEST PARTICIPATES IN THE CEREMONY AT THE GREEK ORTHODOX PATRIARCHATE IN FENER.

AN ADMINISTRATIVE GATHERING IN THE GREEK ORTHODOX PATRIARCHATE IN FENER.

AN ORTHODOX PRIEST DURING A RELIGIOS CEREMONY.

105

106

IN ONE OF THE HISTORICAL ROOMS OF THE ORTHODOX PATRIARCHATE, PICTURES OF ALL THE PATRIARCHS SINCE THE 17th CENTURY DECORATE THE WALLS.

THE MODERN AND THE SPIRITUAL SIDE BY SIDE...

108 THE "ALEVİ" COMMUNITY DEFINES ITSELF WITH ALLEGIANCE TO ALİ, THE COUSIN OF THE PROPHET AND THE FORTH CALIPH. REPRESENTATIONS OF CALIPH ALİ EMBELLISH THE WALLS OF THE ALEVITE "DERGÂH"S (RELIGIOUS CENTERS).

THE ALEVİ COMMUNITY GATHERS FREQUENTLY IN WHAT IS CALLED A "CEM" CEREMONY WHERE
WOMEN AND MEN PRAY TOGETHER.

110 DURING THE "CEM" CEREMONY, THE ALEVİ RELIGIOUS LEADER IS SALUTED BY BELIEVERS IN THE TRADITIONAL WAY.

ART OF SOCIALIZING

HOSPITABLE

PEOPLE OF İSTANBUL HAVE PERFECTED THE
ART OF SOCIALIZING AND BOARD GAMES ARE
AN ESSENTIAL INGREDIENT. ANY
GARDEN CAFÉ SHOULD OFFER BACKGAMMON
BOARDS FOR FREE. AS FOR THOSE IN
CULINARY PURSUIT, THE LOCAL TURKISH
CUISINE IN İSTANBUL IS A CONSTANT ENRICH-
MENT. THE RICH VARIETY BROUGHT TOGETHER
AND REFINED IN THE EMPERIAL KITCHENS
PROVIDES ENOUGH MATERIAL FOR LIFE-LONG
STUDY AND ENJOYMENT.

THE 600 OTTOMAN YEARS LED
TO THE EVOLUTION OF A GRAND
CUISINE THROUGH A LONG
PROCESS OF DIFFERENTIATION
AND PERFECTION. IBN HALDUN'S
WORDS, "THE RELIGION OF THE
KING, IN TIME, BECOMES THAT
OF THE PEOPLE", ALSO
HOLDS FOR FOOD. AND DON'T
FORGET THAT SHOPPING IN THE
THOUSANDS OF SHOPS OF THE
KAPALIÇARŞI (COVERED/GRAND
BAZAAR) AND MISIR ÇARŞISI
(EGYPTIAN MARKET OR SPICE
BAZAAR) QUALIFIES AS EXERCISE,
SO HAVE AN ANOTHER PIECE
OF BAKLAVA.

112 NARGİLE (WATER PIPE OR HUBBLE-BUBBLE) AT ONE SIDE, ATTENTION FOCUSED ON THE "TAVLA" (BACKGAMMON)... TYPICAL TURKISH STYLE!

YOU MAY NOT WANT TO BUY THESE HAND-WOVEN CLOTHES; BUT PLEASE ENTER FOR THE SAKE OF A WARM CHAT.

113

"KAPALIÇARŞI", THE COVERED BAZAAR IS STILL LIKE A SCENE FROM 1001 NIGHTS.
WHATEVER NEEDED IS OFFERED HERE, WHATEVER IS NOT NEEDED IS BOUGHT HERE.

WHILE TRADITIONAL CAFÉS ARE STILL FREQUENTED BY MOSTLY THE MALE POPULATION,
PATISSERIES ARE MORE COSMOPOLITAN.

IT IS NOT EASY, BUT YOU CAN STILL HOPE TO FIND A TABLE OUTDOORS AND ENJOY THE COLOURFUL CROWD OF THE İSTİKLÂL AVENUE, WHICH IS RESERVED FOR PEDESTRIANS.

FRESH FISH FROM THE MEDITERRANEAN, MARMARA AND THE AEGEAN SEAS ARE FOUND IN
MANY PARTS OF THE CITY; BUT THE MOST ENTERTAINING AREA TO BUY FISH IS THE FISH
MARKET IN GALATASARAY.

117

STILL DIETING? FORGET IT! THE SWEETS HERE ARE NOT LIGHT AT ALL. PERHAPS YOU CAN REWARD YOURSELF AFTER A LONG DIET.

THE CHEAPEST AND MOST DELICIOUS BREAKFAST OR QUICKEST LUNCH IS A "SİMİT" (RING-SHAPED
SAVOURY ROLL COVERED WITH SESAME SEEDS) TOGETHER WITH TEA.

IF YOU ARE NOT SATISFIED WITH A "SİMİT" LUNCH, HOW ABOUT DÖNER? IT STANDS AND TURNS IN FRONT OF YOU IN EVERY CORNER OF THE CITY. CHOOSE ONE: BEEF OR CHICKEN.

AS IF ITS CITIZENS FEEL HUNGRY THROUGHOUT THE DAY, THE STREETS OF THE CITY ARE READY TO FULFILL ALL POSSIBLE DEMANDS OF FOOD. HERE IS THE SUMMER MENU: WOULD YOU LIKE YOUR CORN GRILLED OR BOILED?

MODERN ELECTRICAL GRINDERS ARE NOT APPRECIATED BY TURKISH COFFEE MAKERS. YOU HAVE TO USE THE BRASS MILLS TO ACHIEVE THE CORRECT TASTE.

HE IS NOT MEXICAN, NOR IS HE A BELLY DANCER. HE IS JUST ONE OF THE STREET VENDORS OF İSTANBUL, PREPARING AN OLD SWEET CALLED "MACUN" (A GUM-LIKE CANDY).

HE IS NOT POSING FOR THE PHOTOGRAPHERS, BUT FOR THE PIGEONS.

ALL KINDS OF SPICES: FROM MADAGASCAR OR INDIA, FROM THE BLACK SEA COAST OR THE
TOROS MOUNTAINS. THE PLACE IS THE SPICE BAZAAR.

126

IF YOU DO NOT KNOW WHAT TO DO WITH THEM, ASK THE VENDORS. THEY HAVE GOOD RECIPES.

JARRED FRUITS AND VEGETABLES ARE READY TO BE SOLD. IT IS NOT A SHOP'S WINDOW; IT IS THE
DISPLAY CABINET OF THE FAMOUS TRADITIONAL RESTAURANT, "HACI ABDULLAH".

A TEA CENTER IN A BUILDING. TEA CAN BE SERVED AND FOUND EVERYWHERE. ANYWHERE IN THE CITY, TO MURMUR "ÇAY" (PRONOUNCED TCHAI) IS ENOUGH TO SAVOUR A GLASS FULL OF BLACK TEA.

HISTORICAL PERA PALACE HOTEL IS FAMOUS WITH ITS DECORATION AND WORLDWIDE-KNOWN VISITORS.

THE BAR OF PERA PALACE HOTEL IS A TYPICAL COMBINATION OF OTTOMAN AND WESTERN TASTES.

THE MYSTERIOUS ROOM OF THE MYSTERIOUS AUTHOR, AGATHA CHRISTIE, WHO PAID A VISIT TO PERA PALACE HOTEL TO WRITE ONE OF HER TIMELESS MYSTERY NOVELS: "MURDER ON THE ORIENT EXPRESS".

ATATÜRK, SHAH RIZA PEHLEVI, KING EDWARD VIII, PRESIDENT TITO, JACQUELINE KENNEDY, GISCARD D'ESTAING, VON PAPEN, MATA HARI, AGATHA CHRISTIE, YEHUDI MENUHIN, GRETA GARBO...THE VISITOR LIST OF PERA PALACE IS LONGER, BUT WE KNOW THAT ALL OF THEM USED THE SAME ELEVATOR...

132 IN THE SPICE BAZAAR, FAR FROM THE CROWDS, THERE IS A CORNER WHERE FINE TURKISH FOOD IS PRODUCED: THE PLACE IS PANDELİ.

IMACULATE WHITE TABLE CLOTHES, EXQUISITE DISHES, SERIOUS SERVICE... AND LITTLE BIT OF
BUSINESS TALK. THIS IS LUNCH IN A CLASSICAL TURKISH RESTAURANT.

134 IT IS CERTAINLY BORING TO LOOK AT THE FEET AND THE SHOES ALL THE TIME. SOME NICE PHOTOGRAPHS WILL CHEER THE CUSTOMERS UP WHILE THEIR SHOES ARE BEING POLISHED.

HE DOES NOT LIKE VARIETY. HE BELIEVES THAT ONE FINE LADY IS ENOUGH TO PLEASE THE EYES
OF ALL HIS CUSTOMERS.

AFTER A LONG WASH AND MASSAGE, ONE MAY NEED TO REST ALL ALONE IN A SILENT CORNER. THIS CORNER OF THE HAMAM IS CALLED "HALVET".

SILENT…HUMID…WARM…RELAXING…THE BODY IS MUCH MORE IMPORTANT THAN THE SOUL IN
THE HAMAM.

138 "BELLY DANCING IS WONDERFUL, WOULD YOU LIKE TO TRY?"

CRUSADERS AND JANISSARIES

HISTORIC

ITS SKYLINE STUDDED WITH DOMES AND MINARETS, AND STRADDLING THE MYSTICAL BOSPHORUS, İSTANBUL IS ONE THE GREAT ROMANTIC CITIES. ITS HISTORY IS FULL OF ECHOS FROM BYZANTIUM AND THE OTTOMAN EMPIRE. IN THIS SPRAWLING, CONTINENT-SPANNING CITY YOU CAN TRAMP THE STREETS WHERE CRUSADERS AND JANISSARIES ONCE MARCHED; ADMIRE MOSQUES AS THE MOST SUBLIME ARCHITECTURAL EXPRESSIONS OF MUSLIM PIETY; PEER INTO THE SULTAN'S HAREM AND HUNT FOR BARGAINS AT THE LOCAL BAZAARS.

UMBERTO ECO EXPRESSES HIS FEELINGS FOR İSTANBUL'S HISTORY AS FOLLOWS: "I COULD NO LONGER TELL IF I WAS IN BYZANTIUM, CONSTATINOPOLIS OR İSTANBUL. I REALIZED THAT I MADE A TRIP WHERE I TRAVERSED THREE CIVILIZATIONS AND THREE PERIODS AT THE SAME TIME. BUT THIS CITY WITH THREE NAMES AND THREE HISTORIES WAS IN FACT STILL THE SAME. I THOUGHT THAT IT WAS PERHAPS NOT COINCIDENTAL THAT AMIDST THE CITY WALLS, BEARDED CHURCH FATHERS HAD DISCUSSED TO THE POINT OF EXHAUSTION THE SECRET OF THE TRINITY, THAT IS HOW ONE THING COULD BE AT ONCE ONE AND THREE"*

*ATLAS MAGAZINE, 1999, SPECIAL ISSUE.

140 İSTANBUL IS A CITY OF MINARETS, LIGHTHOUSES AND TOWERS. ONE IS THE MAIDEN'S TOWER (KIZ KULESİ) ON AN ISLET AT THE MOUTH OF THE BOSPHORUS WHICH STILL SERVES AS A LIGHTHOUSE SINCE THE 12th CENTURY.

BUILT IN MID 15th CENTURY BY MEHMET THE CONQUEROR, RUMELİ HİSARI (RUMELİ FORTRESS),
STANDS NOBLY ON THE EUROPEAN SIDE OF THE BOSPHORUS.

142 ON THE OTHER SIDE OF THE BOSPHORUS, ANADOLU HİSARI (ANATOLIAN FORTRESS) THE ELDER SISTER OF RUMELİ HİSARI, STANDS MORE HUMBLY.

THE ÇIRAĞAN PALACE, A RESIDENCE OF THE OTTOMAN SULTANS IN THE 19th CENTURY, HAS BEEN RESTORED TO ITS FORMER GLORY AND NOW SERVES AS A LUXURY HOTEL ON THE EUROPEAN SHORES OF THE BOSPHORUS.

144   THE KÜÇÜKSU PAVILLION, DESIGNED BY THE ARCHITECT BALYAN AND COMPLETED IN 1857, STANDS ON THE ASIAN SHORES OF THE BOSPHORUS. IT IS BEING RESTORED AND WILL SOON BE AVAILABLE FOR PRIVATE RECEPTIONS.

ALSO DESIGNED BY THE OTTOMAN ARCHITECT BALYAN, THE BEYLERBEYİ PALACE (1861-1865) WAS GENERALLY RESERVED FOR SUMMER USE BY THE SULTANS OR TO ACCOMMODATE FOREIGN HEADS OF STATE VISITING THE OTTOMAN CAPITAL.

146 FORMER RESIDENCES OF THE ARISTOCRACY DURING THE LAST YEARS OF THE OTTOMAN EMPIRE ARE NOW UNDER LEGAL PROTECTION.

SÜLEYMANİYE MOSQUE DOMINATES A PART OF THE SILHOUETTE OF THE OLD TOWN REFLECTING
THE ARCHITECTURAL PERFECTION THAT THE OTTOMAN EMPIRE AND ITS GREATEST ARCHITECT
SİNAN HAD REACHED.

148

WHEN CONSTANTINOPLE BECAME İSTANBUL AND THE OTTOMANS GAINED CONTROL, SİNAN DESIGNED THE SÜLEYMANİYE COMPLEX FOR THE SULTAN SÜLEYMAN THE MAGNIFICENT AND THE LAWGIVER. THE COMPLEX, CALLED "KÜLLİYE" WAS FINISHED IN 1557, THE MOSQUE BEING THE FOCUS OF THE COMPLEX.

KULELİ MILITARY HIGH SCHOOL, BUILT AT THE END OF 19th CENTURY, IS SITUATED AT THE ASIAN SIDE OF THE BOSPHORUS EMBELLISHING THE AREA WITH ITS DIGNIFIED VIEW. THE TOWERS OF THE BUILDING ARE LIKE TWO BROTHERS WEARING CONICAL CAPS TO PROTECT THEM FROM THE SUN.

149

150

İSTANBUL IS KNOWN FOR THE BEAUTIFUL RESIDENCES THAT LINE BOTH SIDES OF THE BOSPHORUS. THEY WERE BUILT IN HARMONY WITH THE NATURAL ENVIRONMENT AND THUS APPEAR AS IF THEY ARE A PART OF THE VERY FABRIC OF THE MEANDERING WATERSIDE.

GALATA TOWER IS NOW AN IMPORTANT ATTRACTION FOR TOURISTS. BUT IT HAS SERVED A FEW OTHER INTERESTS TOO. IN THE 17th CENTURY AHMET ÇELEBİ, A TURKISH DAREDEVIL, LAUNCHED HIS HANG-GLIDER FROM THE TOP AND FLEW ACROSS THE BOSPHORUS, BECOMING THE FIRST MAN TO FLY SINCE THE MYTHICAL ICARUS.

152

SELİMİYE BARRACKS WAS BUILT AT THE END OF 19th CENTURY. FLORANCE NIGHTINGALE, THE LADY OF THE LAMP, HURRIED FROM ONE TOWER OF THE BARRACKS TO ANOTHER, RELIEVING THE SUFFERING OF THE WOUNDED.

THE TOWERS CLOSEST TO MAIDEN'S TOWER ARE THOSE OF SELİMİYE BARRACKS. THESE TOWERS HAVE NEVER GUIDED SHIPS AT SEA; INSTEAD THEIR LIGHT IS THAT OF FLORENCE NIGHTINGALE, WHO REFORMED THE BRITISH HOSPITAL HERE DURING THE CRIMEAN WAR, AND REVOLUTIONIZED THE NURSING PROFESSION.

154   İSTANBUL ARCHEOLOGY MUSEUM WAS ESTABLISHED BY ARTIST OSMAN HAMDİ BEY AT THE END
OF THE 19th AT THE END OF THE 19th CENTURY. ITS ARCHITECT WAS VALLAURY. BESIDES BEING
THE FIRST TURKISH MUSEUM, IT IS ONE OF THE FEW BUILDINGS IN THE WORLD BUILT AS A
MUSEUM.

NOT MANY UNIVERSITY CAMPUSES CAN BOAST OF BEING SITUATED ON WHAT WAS ONCE ONE OF THE ANCIENT WORLD'S GREAT CENTERS OF POWER. İSTANBUL UNIVERSITY CAN. ITS MAIN CAMPUS STANDS ON THE GROUNDS OF THE FIRST PALACE OF OTTOMAN RULER MEHMET II.

156 SITUATED NEAR THE GALATA BRIDGE, PRACTICALLY IN THE SHADOW OF THE NEW MOSQUE, IS THE FAMOUS EGYPTIAN SPICE BAZAAR (MISIR ÇARŞISI). MUCH SMALLER THAN THE GRAND BAZAAR AND SLIGHTLY LESS TOURISTIC, THE SPICE BAZAAR WAS BUILT IN 1660 TO HELP SUPPORT THE UPKEEP OF THE MOSQUE.

THE SURREALISTIC ATMOSPHERE OF THE UNDERGROUND CISTERN IS FASCINATING. IT WAS BUILT BY BYZANTINE EMPEROR JUSTINIAN IN THE 6th CENTURY. IN TURKISH, IT IS CALLED "YEREBATAN SARAYI" MEANING "UNDERGROUND PALACE."

158

ST. IRENE, LOCATED IN THE FIRST COURTYARD AT TOPKAPI PALACE, IS THE FIRST BYZANTINE CHURCH OF İSTANBUL. IT WAS BUILT BY CONSTANTINE IN THE 4th CENTURY. JUSTINIAN LATER HAD IT RESTAURED. IT IS THE ONLY EXAMPLE OF A BYZANTINE CHURCH IN THE CITY THAT RETAINS AN ORIGINAL ATRIUM. TODAY IT SERVES MAINLY AS A CONCERT HALL. MEHMET THE CONQUEROR'S CHRISTIAN STEP MOTHER PRAYED INTHIS CHURCH. TODAY IT STANDS AS A REMINDER OF RELIGIOUS TOLERANCE.

BUILT BETWEEN 1597 AND 1663, THE YENİ (NEW) MOSQUE HOVERS OVER THE HARBOR AT
EMİNÖNÜ OVERLOOKING THE FERRYBOATS COMING TO THE OLD PART OF THE CITY. THE
MOSQUE WAS ORIGINALLY COMMISSIONED BY SULTAN MEHMET III IN MEMORY OF HIS MOTHER.

160 ATATÜRK REGARDED DOLMABAHÇE PALACE AS THE PROPERTY OF A NATION THAT HAD EXCHANGED THE RULE OF A SULTAN FOR THAT OF A REPUBLICAN ADMINISTRATION. HE CHOSE DOLMABAHÇE PALACE AS HIS RESIDENCE DURING HIS VISITS TO İSTANBUL. HIS ROOM HAS REMAINED THE SAME SINCE HIS DEATH THERE.

DOLMABAHÇE PALACE, BUILT IN THE MIDDLE OF 19th CENTURY, IS A THREE-STORY STRUCTURE. THERE IS A CLEAR WESTERN INFLUENCE IN ITS DESIGN, DETAIL AND ORNAMENTATION, BUT THE BUILDING IS A WORK OF OTTOMAN ARCHITECTS' MASTERLY INTERPRETATION OF THESE IMPRESSIONS.

TODAY ALL SECTIONS OF DOLMABAHÇE PALACE ARE RESTORED AND OPEN TO VISITORS. THERE IS A PERMANENT EXHIBITION OF A COLLECTION OF ARCHITECTURAL ORNAMENTATIONS AND VARIOUS PALACE ITEMS AND OBJECTS.

THE COVE, WHICH WAS A NATURAL HARBOR WHERE THE OTTOMAN ADMIRALS ANCHORED THE NAVAL FLEET, HAD BEGUN TO SILT UP FROM TIME TO TIME AND BECAME ONE OF THE UNIQUE GARDENS OF THE BOSPHORUS CALLED DOLMABAHÇE (FILLED GARDEN).

DOLMABAHÇE WAS BUILT ON A SITE OF MORE THAN 110,000 SQUARE METERS AND CONSISTS OF 16 SECTIONS IN ADDITION TO THE MAIN STRUCTURE. THE PALACE HALLS ARE FURNISHED TO EMPHASIZE THE HISTORICAL SPLENDOR OF THE EMPIRE.

OVER THE YEARS, DOLMABAHÇE WAS DEVELOPED AS A SERIES OF VILLAS AND PAVILIONS BUILT BY VARIOUS SULTANS. IT EVENTUALLY BEGAN TO LOOK LIKE "BEŞİKTAŞ WATERSIDE PALACE."

166

DOLMABAHÇE PALACE WAS CONSTRUCTED BY THE FOREMOST OTTOMAN ARCHITECTS OF THE PERIOD KARABET AND NIKOGOS BALYAN. THE MAIN BLOCK OF THE PALACE IS COMPOSED OF THREE SECTIONS, NAMELY; THE MABEYN-I HÜMAYUN/ SELAMLIK (MEN'S SECTION), THE CEREMONIAL HALL AND THE HAREM.

BEING A CAT IN FRONT OF AN IMPERIAL PALACE, LOOKING AT THE SCULPTORS OF ITS
ANCESTORS DOESN'T SEEM SO BAD, DOES IT?

168

THE FOUNTAIN OF AHMET III, BUILT IN 1728, IS ARGUABLY ONE OF THE MOST HANDSOME PUBLIC FOUNTAINS ANYWHERE IN THE WORLD, IS SITUATED IN BETWEEN TOPKAPI PALACE AND AYA SOFYA (ST. SOPHIA).

İSTANBUL: CITY OF MEMORIES & HOPES

COLORFUL AND EXOTIC

ENTERTAINING

İSTANBUL IS A CITY FOR WALKING AND GAZING. BUT
INSTEAD OF WHIRLING LIKE A DERVISH, IT IS BETTER
TO DIVIDE AND CONQUER THE CITY'S ATTRACTIONS.
İSTANBUL WAS THE FOCAL POINT FOR THE FORCES
OF WESTERNIZATION THAT TRANSFORMED
POLITICAL AND ECONOMIC INSTITUTIONS AS WELL
AS DOMESTIC LIFE IN TURKEY.

THE CITY AND ITS PEOPLE EXHIBIT A
DISTINCT VARIETY OF COLORS. YOU
CAN SOMETIMES HEAR İSTANBUL
PEOPLE COMPLAINING ABOUT THE
CITY'S MORE-THAN-NECESSARY
DYNAMISM; BUT IF YOU LOOK
THEM CAREFULLY AT THE
FACE, YOU WILL SEE THAT
THEY TRULY ENJOY BEING
AND LIVING IN THIS
WONDERFUL CITY.

170

THE GALATA BRIDGE OFFERS HOPES. THEY HOPE TO FISH FOR "İSTAVRİT" (HORSE MACKEREL).

HE HAS EVERYTHING HE NEEDS IN ORDER TO TO FISH: HOOKS, LINE, A PORTABLE STOOL AND A
PACK OF CIGARETTES.

YOU CAN BE CERTAIN THAT NOT EVERYBODY IS BUYING SPICES. AFTER ALL, THE SPICE BAZAAR IS FUN.

ROBINSON CRUSOE: ONE OF THE MOST ELEGANT BOOKSTORE IN İSTANBUL.

174 PROMOTING "INTERNATIONAL UFO MUSEUM" ON THE İSTİKLÂL, HE CERTAINLY DESERVES A CIGARETTE
BREAK ACCOMPANIED BY A HUMAN BEING.

THEY WERE PLAYING COWBOYS AND INDIANS A LITTLE WHILE AGO. NOW, A BREAK FOR CANDIED APPLES.

176   "BUT YOU HAVE TO SMILE LIKE MARILYN MONROE..."

"BEFORE THE MOVIE, TAKE MY PICTURE!"

AN ELEGANT TRAP FOR WOMEN...

TOYS FOR BOYS ON THE RIGHT SIDE, DOLLS FOR GIRLS ON THE LEFT.

180 ORTAKÖY: A POPULAR MELTING POT.

HE WILL GIVE YOU A TEDDY BEAR IF YOU CAN SHOOT THE RED BALLOON.

HE LIKES FISHING AND SHE LIKES EATING FRESH FISH.

THEY ARE PROTECTING EACH OTHER AGAINST THE DANGERS OF İSTANBUL STREETS.

TATOO... TABOO...

WHILE ICECREAM MELTS IT ALSO COOLS ONE'S MOOD.

THIS IS NOT A COSTUME, IT IS A CLEVER WAY TO SELL BADGES.

HOW ELSE COULD HE BE RECOGNIZED AMONG THE COLORFUL CROWDS?

THE MONUMENT IN TAKSİM SQUARE DOES NOT ALWAYS WITNESS OFFICIAL CEREMONIES…

HE AND HIS HORSE, A PERFECT TEAM.

189

190   THE PRINCE'S ISLANDS ARE FREE FROM CAR TRAFFIC, SO THE HORSES ARE FREE TO RUN.

SPRING MEANS PICNICS IN THE BELGRAD FOREST; PICNICS MEAN SWINGING.

191

192 REPAIRING THE NETS IS ESSENTIAL TO A GOOD CATCH.

"HOW TIRESOME TO REPAIR THE NETS."

194 THE BOATS AND THEIR OWNERS ARE WAITING FOR THE SUN TO SHINE ON THE MYSTERY OF THE BOSHPORUS.

ORTAKÖY SQUARE OFFERS ALTERNATIVES: CATCHING FISH, EATING OR PEOPLE WATCHING.

196   THE BEBEK BAY ON THE BOSPHORUS IS EVERYBODY'S FAVORITE.

"TURYOL" IS THE NATIONAL SYMBOL AND "COM.TR" IS THE GLOBAL MARK OF THEIR BUSINESS.

198

FOR MANY PEOPLE LIVING IN OR VISITING İSTANBUL, NIGHT LIFE DOES NOT MEAN ANYTHING WITHOUT THE GYPSIES. AND GYPSIES KNOW IT VERY WELL!

THE BITTER EXPRESSION ON HIS FACE CAN BE EXPLAINED AWAY: HE IS GOING TO BE CIRCUMCISED.

THE BEST PICNICS ARE IN THE PRINCE'S ISLANDS. THE BEST PICNIC FOOD IS SHISH KEBAB.

SOME LIKE IT PRIVATE.

THE STAGE OF THE GALATASARAY HIGH SCHOOL, GOOD PLACE TO SEE YOUNG ACTORS AND ACRESSES.

THEY ARE PLAYING WITH A WHITE BALLOON IN FRONT OF THE GATE OF A FOOTBALL STADIUM.

204 THE INSTRUMENT IS TRADITIONAL, THE RIG IS HIGH-TECH.

PHOTOGRAPHER'S INDEX

ISTANBUL: CITY OF MEMORIES & HOPES